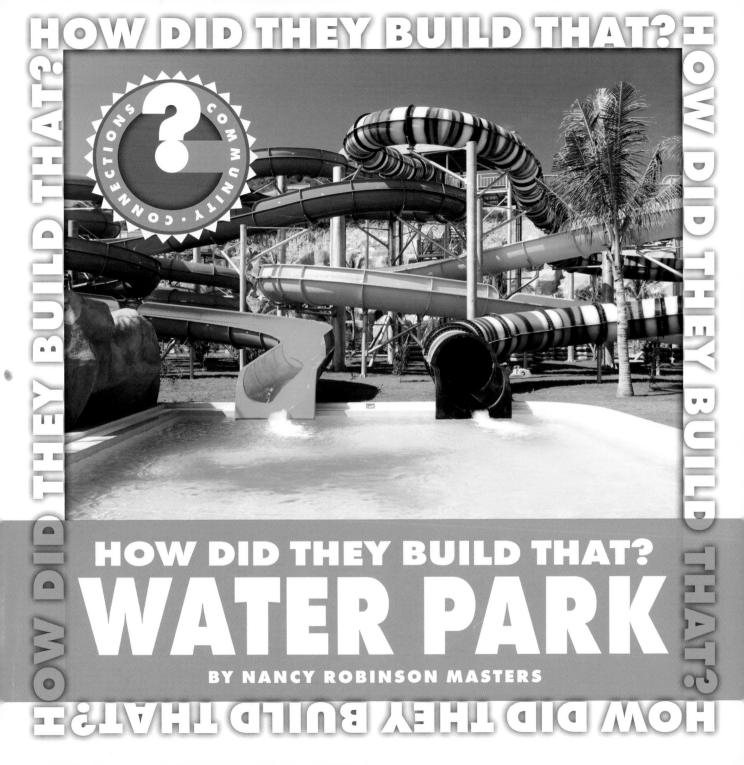

COMMUNITY · CONNECTIONS

?

HOW DID THEY BUILD THAT?
WATER PARK

BY NANCY ROBINSON MASTERS

Published in the United States of America by Cherry Lake Publishing
Ann Arbor, Michigan
www.cherrylakepublishing.com

Content Adviser: Melinda Kempfer, Business Development, Water Technology Inc.,

Photo Credits: Cover and page 1, ©Nikolay Okhitin/Shutterstock, Inc.; page 5, ©karnizz/
Shutterstock, Inc.; page 7, ©iStockphoto.com/orhancam; page 9, ©fotum/Shutterstock, Inc.;
page 11, ©Andresr/Shutterstock, Inc.; page 13, ©Krzysztof Slusarczyk/Shutterstock, Inc.;
page 15, ©oriontrail/Shutterstock, Inc.; page 17, ©iStockphoto.com/DanDriedger; page 19,
©iStockphoto.com/teoden; page 21, ©Ramzi Hachicho/Shutterstock, Inc.

LIBRARY OF CONGRESS CATALOGING-IN-PUBLICATION DATA
Masters, Nancy Robinson.
  Water park/by Nancy Robinson Masters.
    p. cm.—(How did they build that?)
  Includes bibliographical references and index.
  ISBN-13: 978-1-60279-983-7 (lib. bdg.)
  ISBN-10: 1-60279-983-0 (lib. bdg.)
  1. Swimming pools—Design and construction—Juvenile literature. 2. Amusement parks—
Design and construction—Juvenile literature. I. Title.
  TH4763.M37 2011
  725'.76—dc22   2010031627

Cherry Lake Publishing would like to acknowledge the
work of The Partnership for 21st Century Skills. Please
visit www.21stcenturyskills.org for more information.

Printed in the United States of America
Corporate Graphics Inc.
January 2011
CLSP08

WATER PARK

CONTENTS

Developers build water parks indoors and outdoors. They create water parks near malls and motels. Some are built near rivers and lakes. You will even find some water parks on ships.

Some outdoor water parks are very big.

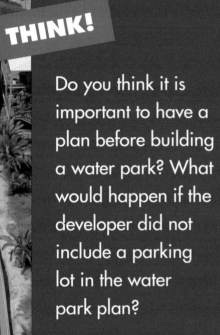

THINK!

Do you think it is important to have a plan before building a water park? What would happen if the developer did not include a parking lot in the water park plan?

Designers plan the water park's theme. They plan the **attractions** to go with the theme. Water slides and splash pools are two main attractions. Inner tube river rides are popular, too.

Designers also decide where restrooms and changing areas will be. They design eating areas and parking lots. They make sure the water park will be fun for everyone.

Designers think of ways to build water parks that are fun for everyone.

Engineers study the plans. They use math and science skills. They have to be sure the attractions are the right shapes and sizes. Engineers make sure the attractions meet **building codes** for safety.

Engineers make sure water park attractions will be safe.

PIPES AND PUMPS

What is the most important water park attraction? Water! Big water parks use millions of gallons of water.

Workers lay large pipes to bring the water to the building site. They lay smaller pipes through the water park. Pumps push water through the smaller pipes to the attractions.

Big pumps keep water moving through water park pipes.

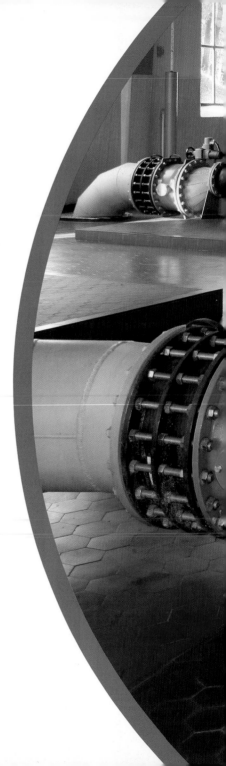

Workers install pumps with filters to **recycle** the water. The filters remove trash and **bacteria**. The recycled water is now clean and safe to use again.

Construction workers use machines to dig holes for splash pools. Some workers run wires and set timers. Other workers test the pumps. Inspectors make sure there are no leaks.

Workers use large machines to dig pools and lay pipes.

Plan your own backyard water park. What can you use to create a water attraction? Be sure it is safe and fun. Wear your swimsuit as you plan.

MAKING A SPLASH

Attractions such as tall slides are built in factories. Then they are moved to the water park. Other attractions are built at the water park.

Computers control some of the attractions. Workers use computers to start big fans. The fans help make the waves in wave pools.

Many water parks have wave pools.

Some computers help open and close gates. This helps control crowds. It also moves visitors to attractions quickly.

Have you ever seen a robot swim? Water park robots can! They are used to clean the bottoms of pools.

Clean water is important in a water park. Robots you can't see may be used to help clean pools.

Most water park attractions are made of **fiberglass**. It is strong and molds easily into different shapes. It takes months to build all of the attractions.

Water parks add new attractions every year. This keeps people coming back for more fun!

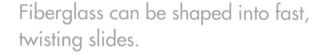

Fiberglass can be shaped into fast, twisting slides.

You don't have to go to a water park to find objects made of fiberglass. Look for things in your house that are made of fiberglass. Ask an adult to help you. Some objects are so small you might need a magnifying glass!

GLOSSARY

amusement park (uh-MYOOS-muhnt PARK) a park with attractions where people go to have fun

attractions (uh-TRAK-shunz) fun things to see and do in a water park

bacteria (bak-TEER-ee-uh) tiny living things that cause sickness

building codes (BILL-ding KOHDZ) rules for building things safely

designers (duh-ZY-nurz) people who create water park plans

developers (duh-VEH-luh-purz) people who decide what kind of water park to build and where to build it

engineers (en-jih-NEERZ) people who help plan and build water parks

fiberglass (FIE-bur-glass) a building material made of a kind of glass and used in water parks

recycle (ree-SY-kuhl) to use again

FIND OUT MORE

BOOKS

Irving, Dianne. *Amusement Parks*. Huntington Beach, CA: Teacher Created Materials, 2009.

Masters, Nancy Robinson. *How Did That Get to My House? Water.* Ann Arbor: Cherry Lake Publishing, 2010.

WEB SITES

Explore the Park—LEGOLAND
california.legoland.com/Explore
Explore a water park with a construction theme.

Waterparks.com
www.waterparks.com/funfacts.asp
Learn about water parks around the world.

INDEX

ABOUT THE AUTHOR

Nancy Robinson Masters is the author of more than 35 books. She is also an airplane pilot. She and her husband, Bill, like to fly their airplane to visit water parks in Texas. What attraction do you think they like best at a water park?